In the Footsteps of Explorers

Ponce de León

Exploring Florida and Puerto Rico

Rachel Eagen

Crabtree Publishing Company

www.crabtreebooks.com

Crabtree Publishing Company
www.crabtreebooks.com

For my parents, Erin and Sheila Eagen

Coordinating editor: Ellen Rodger
Series editor: Carrie Gleason
Editors: Adrianna Morganelli, L. Michelle Nielsen
Design and production coordinator: Rosie Gowsell
Cover design and layout: Samara Parent
Art direction: Rob MacGregor
Scanning technician: Arlene Arch
Photo research: Allison Napier

Consultant: Susan R. Parker, PhD., historian

Photo Credits: The Art Archive/ Science Academy Lisbon/ Dagli Orti: p. 5; British Library, London, UK/ Bridgeman Art Library: p. 8; Service Historique de la Marine, Vincennes, France, Lauros, Giraudon/ Brideman Art Library: p. 24, p. 25 (top); Bettmann/ Corbis: pp. 12 – 13; Wolfgang Kaehler/ Corbis: p. 31; Danny Lehman/ Corbis: p. 11; Amos Nachoum/ Corbis: p. 15; Nik Wheeler/ Corbis: p. 30; Suzanne Murphy/ DDB Stock: pp. 22 – 23; Tina Chambers/ Dorling Kindersley: p. 20 (right); Getty Images: cover; istock International: p. 21; North Wind Picture Archive: p. 6, p. 7 (bottom), p. 9, p. 16, p. 17, p. 19, p.26, p. 29; Other images from stock photo cd

Illustrations: Lauren Fast: p. 7 (top); Roman Goforth: p. 4; David Wysotski: pp. 20-21

Cartography: Jim Chernishenko: title page, p. 10, p. 28

Cover: According to legend, Ponce de León searched for the Fountain of Youth in Florida. He did not find it, as no such magical waters exists.

Title page: Ponce de León traveled from Spain to Hispaniola, an island which includes the present-day countries of Haiti and Dominican Republic. He then explored Puerto Rico and the coasts of Florida.

Sidebar icon: Ponce de León and his men tried turtle meat for the first time when they sailed through the turtle-filled islands of Las Tortugas. They removed the shells, and then cut the meat into long slices. The meat was salted and hung to dry in the sea air. When it had dried, the crew ate the meat as turtle jerky.

Crabtree Publishing Company
www.crabtreebooks.com 1-800-387-7650

Printed in Canada/112019/EF2019027

Library of Congress Cataloging-in-Publication Data
Eagen, Rachel, 1979-
Ponce de León : exploring Florida and Puerto Rico / written by Rachel Eagen.
p. cm. -- (In the footsteps of explorers)
Includes index.
ISBN-13: 978-0-7787-2412-4 (rlb)
ISBN-10: 0-7787-2412-3 (rlb)
ISBN-13: 978-0-7787-2448-3 (pbk)
ISBN-10: 0-7787-2448-4 (pbk)
1. Ponce de León, Juan, 1460-1521--Juvenile literature. 2. Explorers --America--Biography--Juvenile literature. 3. Explorers--Spain--Biography --Juvenile literature. 4. Florida--Discovery and exploration--Spanish --Juvenile literature. 5. Puerto Rico--Discovery and exploration--Spanish --Juvenile literature. I. Title. II. Series.
E125.P7E23 2005
972.9'02'092--dc22 [B] 2005015377
LC

Published in Canada
Crabtree Publishing
616 Welland Ave.
St. Catharines, Ontario
L2M 5V6

Published in the United States
Crabtree Publishing
PMB 59051
350 Fifth Avenue, 59th Floor
New York, New York 10118

Published in the United Kingdom
Crabtree Publishing
Maritime House
Basin Road North, Hove
BN41 1WR

Published in Australia
Crabtree Publishing
Unit 3 – 5
Currumbin Court
Capalaba QLD 4157

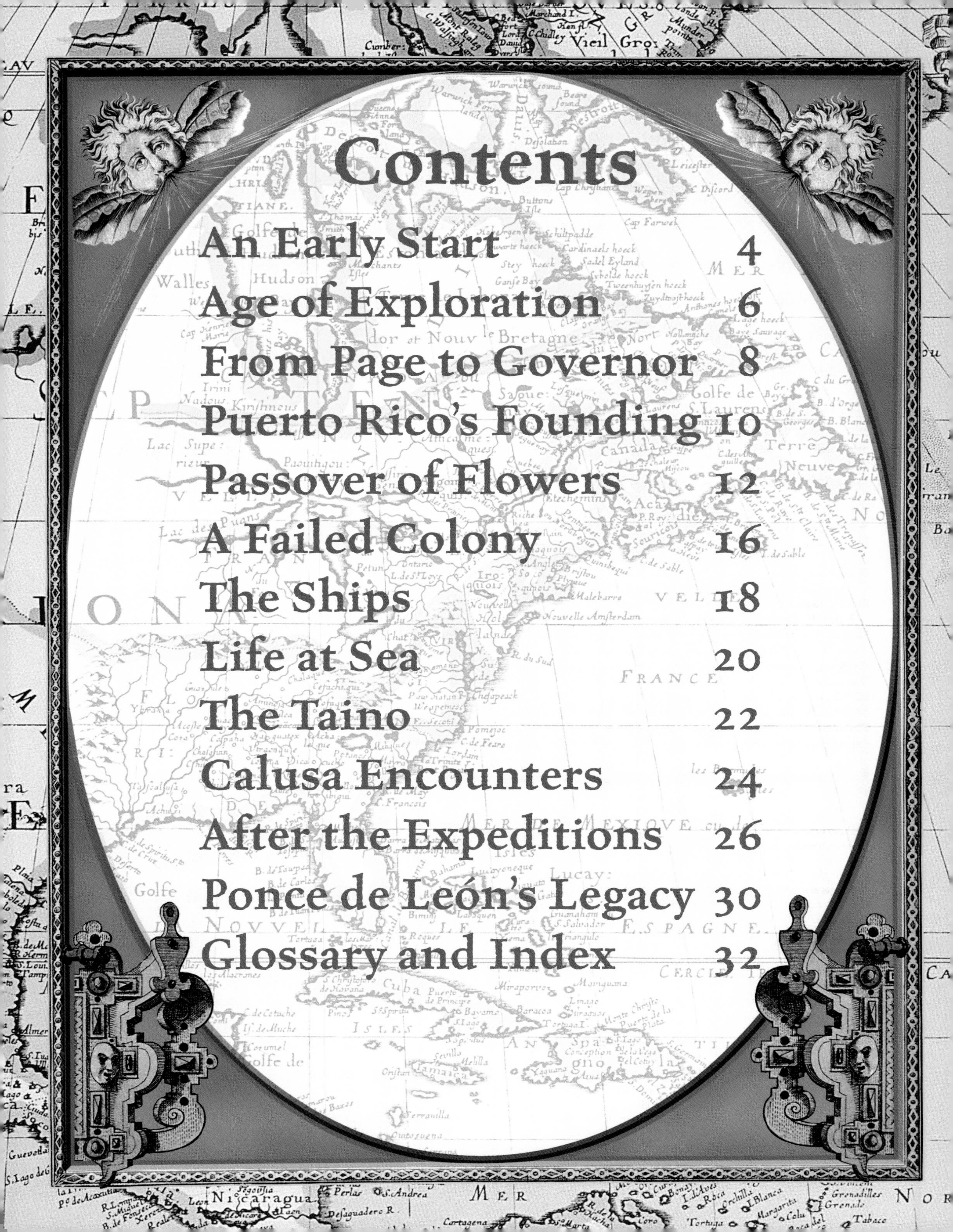
Hudson
Canada
Terre Neuve
FRANCE
Cuba
Nicaragua
Jamaica
Tortuga
Cartagena

Contents

An Early Start

Juan Ponce de León was a Spanish explorer who claimed lands for the Spanish king and queen in the 1500s. He was the first European to establish a colony on what is now known as the island of Puerto Rico. Ponce de León also explored the Florida coast and is credited with the discovery of the Gulf Stream**.**

Farewell Spain

Ponce de León was a teenager when he made his first trip to the **New World**. As an adult, Ponce de León established successful farming **plantations** on some Caribbean Islands. He was also a soldier and leader, who was hired by the king and queen of Spain to put down **rebellions** of native peoples in the New World.

In the Words of...

Ponce de León made two trips to Florida. During the first voyage, Ponce de León and his **pilot** discovered the Gulf Stream and explored the west coast. The second voyage was an attempt to **colonize** the land. According to historian Gonzalo Fernández de Oviedo y Valdés, who met Ponce de León before the second voyage, Ponce de León brought all of the necessary **cargo** for building a permanent settlement.

(above) Ponce de León was respected by the Spanish king and queen for his leadership.

"There were two hundred men and fifty horses aboard the [two] ships...And in order to outfit this armada, a lot [of money] was spent...And as a good colonist, he carried mares and heifers and pigs and sheep and goats and all sorts of useful, domestic animals to serve the people. And also, for agriculture and farming all sorts of seeds were provided, as if the business of his settlement was no more than arriving and cultivating the land and grazing his livestock...This fleet reached that land...and then the governor, Juan Ponce, when he disembarked gave an order, as a man would issue a decree, that the people of his fleet should rest."

- Gonzalo Fernández de Oviedo y Valdés

(below) This historic drawing shows an early settlement in Florida. Ponce de León was the first Spanish explorer in Florida, but his attempt to build a colony there failed.

- 1474 -

Juan Ponce de León born in San Servas, in what is now Spain.

- 1493 -

Ponce de León accompanies explorer Christopher Columbus on a voyage to colonize the Caribbean Islands.

- 1521 -

Ponce de León dies from an infected wound after a battle with Indians in what is now Florida.

Age of Exploration

The discovery of unknown seas and islands provided a new source of wealth for European countries. In the 1400s, many European explorers began traveling further from home in search of riches.

(above) European cities, such as the Portuguese port of Lisbon, prospered from the trade of goods from distant lands. The explorers who discovered the lands also shared in the riches and received positions of power in new colonies.

In the New World

Christopher Columbus, an explorer born in Italy, first visited the islands of the Caribbean for Spain. He found the islands while trying to **navigate** a sea route to the Far East. The Far East, which included China, India, and Japan, was rich with valuable trade goods such as silk, spices, and gold. At the time, trade routes around Africa to the Far East were controlled by Portugal. Columbus thought the islands he stumbled upon were actually part of China. Columbus' mistake encouraged other explorers to claim new lands for their own countries. The period in which European explorers first came to the New World is called the Age of Exploration.

Religion and Exploration

In Spain, a campaign to reclaim Spanish territory that had been taken over by followers of other religions was taking place. The Spanish king and queen were **Christians**. The Moors, a people from Africa who followed the religion of **Islam**, lived in the Spanish province of Granada. The Moors and the Spanish Christians fought each other over the province of Granada for over 700 years. As a result of centuries of fighting in the name of their religion, Spanish explorers, often ex-soldiers, reached new lands desiring to **convert** the people they encountered to Christianity. By spreading their religion, the Spanish felt that they were fulfilling their duty to God.

(below) King Ferdinand and Queen Isabella of Spain were eager to build a Spanish empire in the New World. An empire is made up of one country ruling over the people and resources of other lands.

- 1492 -

Christopher Columbus (above) makes his first voyage to the New World.

- 1519 -

Spanish conquistador, or explorer, Hernando Cortés begins conquering lands in present-day Mexico.

- 1532 -

Spanish conquistador Francisco Pizarro battles the Inca in Peru.

From Page to Governor

Ponce de León was a soldier who fought for the Spanish crown against the Moors in Granada. His hard work helped him advance in rank and to eventually be rewarded as governor **of new lands in the Caribbean.**

Growing Up

Ponce de León was born to a noble Spanish family. Nobles, such as **knights**, were wealthy people who held positions of authority, or power, granted to them by a king or queen. Ponce de León spent most of his youth working as a page for a Spanish knight. As a page, Ponce de León cleaned his knight's clothing, cared for his weapons, and tended his horses. In return, he was taught a code of honor, or the way in which he would be expected to behave, as a knight.

Reclaiming Granada

Ponce de León then became a squire. Squires were taught to hunt and handle weapons such as swords and harquebuses, or Spanish guns that looked like rifles. Ponce de León put his military training to work when he was **recruited** to fight against the Moors in Granada from 1487 to 1492. King Ferdinand and Queen Isabella were impressed by Ponce de León's performance in the war.

(above) Ponce de León's early training as a squire prepared him to be a soldier, and later, a conquistador.

(background) Ponce de León's wealth and success as a soldier allowed him to join Christopher Columbus' second voyage to the New World. In the New World, Ponce de León helped build a settlement called Higüey on the island of Hispaniola. When the Indians of the island revolted against the Spanish colonists, Ponce de León fought to keep order at the settlement. As a reward, the island's governor granted Ponce de León a parcel of land called an encomienda *for farming and a number of Indians to work the land.*

Puerto Rico's Founding

From the Taino Indians of Hispaniola, Ponce de León learned of a nearby island they called Borinquén. Today, Borinquén is known as Puerto Rico.

Borinquén

Ponce de León was eager to explore Borinquén, as it was rumored by the Taino on Hispaniola to be rich in gold. He was granted permission to explore the island from Hispaniola's governor and from King Ferdinand. Explorers needed permission from the crown to explore so that they could officially rule over the new land.

(below) Today, the island of Hispaniola is shared by Haiti and the Dominican Republic.

Caparra

Ponce de León sailed to Puerto Rico and established a settlement on the island called Caparra. He was granted the title of governor of the island. To set up the colony, the Spanish needed the help of the Taino living there. The Spanish recruited Taino to farm the land and to pan the rivers and streams for gold. The Spanish promised to pay the Taino Indians for their work by protecting them from the Carib Indians who lived on islands to the south. The Carib raided Taino villages looking for slaves.

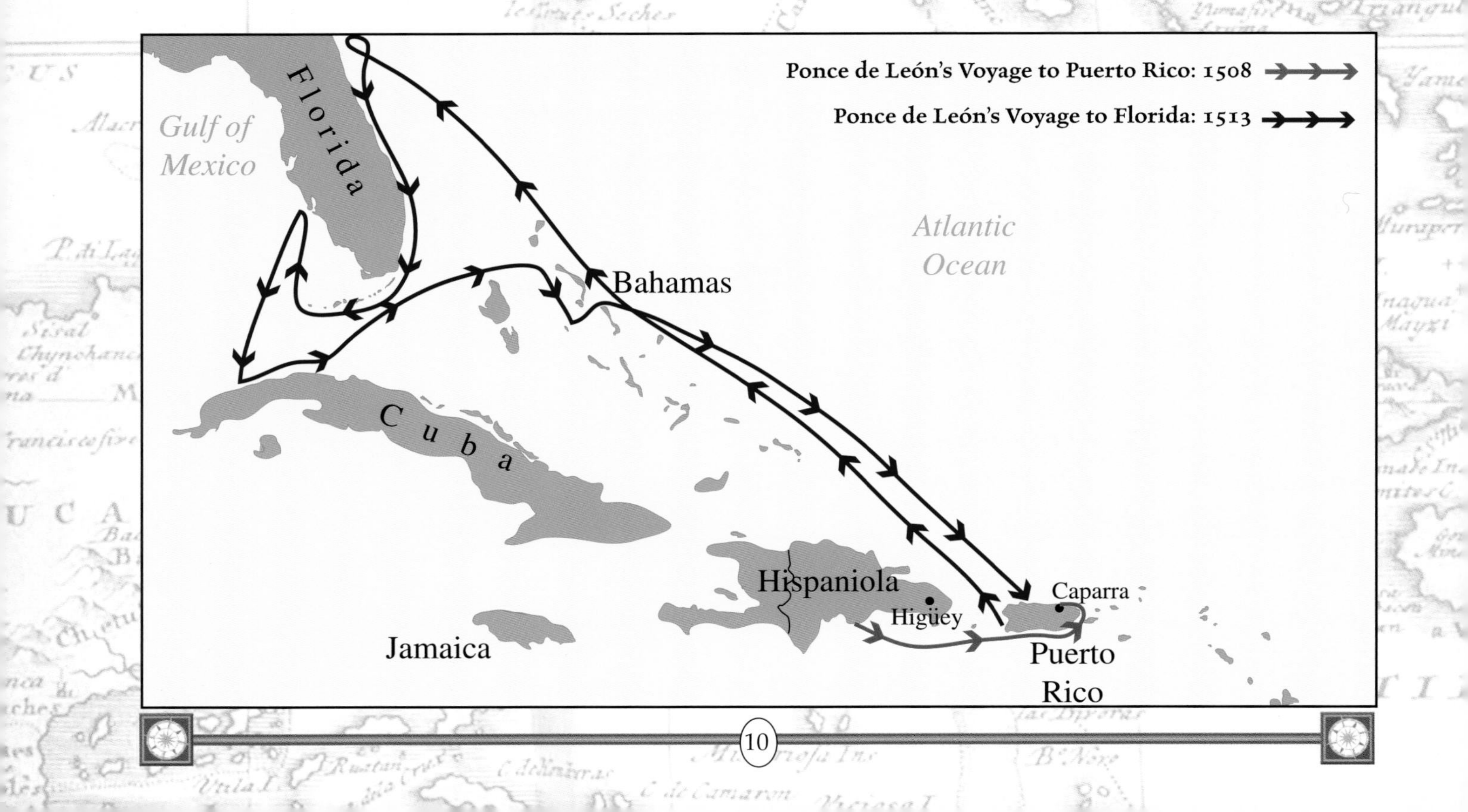

The coastline of Puerto Rico with its sandy beaches and blue ocean.

Living off the Land

Caparra became a successful farming colony. As governor, Ponce de León organized the Taino to help him build stone houses and plant crops. They grew maize and sugar cane, and raised livestock such as pigs and cattle brought by the Spanish. Ponce de León also established a cassava plantation. Cassava, a starchy root native to the island, became a **staple** food crop. It was baked into bread that did not rot over the period of time it took to cross the Atlantic Ocean.

Out of Power

Christopher Columbus had found and claimed Borinquén for Spain during his voyages, but he did not build a settlement there. After his father's death, Diego Columbus began pressuring the Spanish crown to grant him his **inheritance**. As Christopher Columbus' son, Diego was heir to the lands that his father had discovered. After about one year as governor of the island, Ponce de León was replaced by Diego Columbus as Puerto Rico's ruler.

- 1493 -
Ponce de León joins Columbus' second voyage to the New World.

- 1508 -
Juan Ponce granted permission to colonize Puerto Rico.

- 1510 -
Settlement of Caparra, Puerto Rico, completed.

- 1511 -
Juan Ponce replaced by Diego Columbus as governor of Puerto Rico.

Passover of Flowers

No longer governor of Puerto Rico, Ponce de León sent a letter to King Ferdinand asking to explore an island the Taino called Bimini. Ponce de León was anxious to gain the power that he had lost in Caparra. Other explorers had made names for themselves by claiming new lands, but Ponce de León had yet to find lands of his own.

Ready for Push-off

It took Ponce de León one full year to prepare for his expedition to Bimini, because he had to pay for the voyage himself. He loaded his ships with supplies needed for the journey, such as food and gifts to trade with the Indians he and his crew were likely to meet.

Land Ahoy!

Within a month after setting out, Ponce de León and his crew sighted what they thought was a very large island, but was actually the **peninsula** of present-day Florida. Ashore, Ponce de León found an endless stretch of beautiful sandy beach with seashells and bright green vegetation. The land they saw was covered with tropical flowers, butterflies, and birds. Ponce de León claimed the land for Spain and named it La Florida, which is Spanish for "the flowered one." It was Easter, a Christian holiday, when Juan Ponce discovered Florida. The Spanish called the holy day Pascua de Flores, or Feast of Flowers.

(background) Some historians believe King Ferdinand granted Ponce de León permission to explore Florida because he wanted to find the Fountain of Youth. According to legend, the Fountain of Youth was a stream that could make an old person young again by drinking from or bathing in its magical waters. The Taino may have told the explorers about the fountain so they would leave their settlements behind to search for it. Ponce de León never found the Fountain of Youth because it never existed.

Mysterious Waters

Ponce de León and his crew sailed north up Florida's east coast. Ponce de León and his best pilot, Antón de Alaminos, discovered the Gulf Stream, a strong **ocean current** that whips along the coast at about five miles (eight kilometers) per hour. The Gulf Stream moves north up the east coast of North America, then curves toward Europe. Ships sailing on the current reached Europe faster.

Troubles

Ponce de León and his crew tried to go ashore near what some historians believe is now Daytona, Florida. The Indian inhabitants of the area shot arrows at the crew. Ponce de León's ships headed south and rounded the tip of the Florida peninsula and entered the Gulf of Mexico. He sailed west through the area known today as the Florida Keys. Sailing north along the west coast of the Florida peninsula he reached Charlotte Harbor, between present-day Fort Myers and Sarasota. Once again, Ponce de León tried to go ashore but the Calusa Indians would not allow him to.

A Happy King

When Ponce de León finally returned to Spain, he immediately petitioned King Ferdinand for permission to make a second voyage to La Florida. Despite the attack by Calusa Indians, Ponce de León wanted to go back and establish a Spanish colony on the peninsula. He knew that the land was **fertile** because of the vegetation he had discovered growing there, so he believed it would make good farmland. King Ferdinand not only granted Ponce de León permission to establish a colony in Florida, he also named him governor of the land. Ferdinand rewarded Ponce de León by presenting him with a personal **coat-of-arms**.

- March 4, 1513 -
Ponce de León departs Puerto Rico for Florida.

- April 3, 1513 -
Ponce de León reaches the Florida coast.

- October 1513 -
Ponce de León and his crew return to Puerto Rico.

(background) On Ponce de León's way back to Puerto Rico after discovering Florida, he sailed through a cluster of about 70 islands. He claimed these islands for Spain and named them Las Tortugas, which is Spanish for Turtle Islands. Ponce de León and his crew captured and killed more than 160 enormous sea turtles one evening as they sailed around the islands. The islands became known as the Dry Tortugas because they have no fresh water.

A Failed Colony

Ponce de León's return to the New World was delayed by the death of King Ferdinand. Ponce de León stayed in Spain to gain the favor of Spain's new king, Carlos I. Once back in Puerto Rico, Ponce de León was sent to help defend the colony from an attack by Indians.

A New Colony

Ponce de León left Puerto Rico for a second voyage to La Florida on February 20, 1521. His fleet of two ships carried as many as 200 men and women who would live at the new settlement. Ponce de León also brought doctors for healing the sick, and priests for converting the Indians. His cargo included livestock, such as horses, cows, sheep, goats, and pigs, as well as farming tools and seeds. After about three weeks, the crew landed on the Gulf, or west, coast of Florida, between present-day Fort Myers and Charlotte Harbor.

(right) Ponce de León brought 50 horses to Florida. When the Spanish were attacked, the horses were set free. Many people believe these were the first Spanish horses in North America.

Members of the Crew

On the first trip to Florida in 1513, Ponce de León brought two women with him, one of which was named Juana Ruíz. Also among his crew were two free black Africans, two native slaves, and one white slave. The Africans and women were believed to be the first blacks and first European women to set foot in North America.

Attack

Ponce de León and his crew spent up to a few months on the coast, building a permanent settlement. One day, an attack by the local natives, thought by most historians to be the Calusa Indians, took the Spaniards by surprise.

Many Spanish were killed in the attack. Ponce de León was seriously wounded when he was pierced in the thigh by a reed arrow. The rest of the Spanish abandoned the Florida settlement and headed back to Puerto Rico.

(background) Ponce de León's attempt to build a Spanish colony in Florida in 1521 failed. Calusa Indians attacked the Spanish settlers, driving them back to their ships.

The Ships

- Sand glass -
Sailors kept track of the time by turning a sand glass over each time the sand had drained from one funnel to the other.

- Log line -
A length of rope was knotted at equal intervals and used to measure the ship's speed.

Ponce de León led three ships during his voyages. They were called the *Santiago*, the *Santa María de la Consolación*, and the *San Cristóbal*.

Santiago

The *Santiago* was a type of ship called a caravel. Caravels were wide ships built for sailing in the Mediterranean Sea. As Spanish explorers headed further out to sea, they used the caravels because the ships' tall sides made them perfect for fighting the high waves of the stormy Atlantic. Caravels were both light and fast, and they could carry up to 130 tons of cargo. The *Santiago* was about 65 feet (20 meters) long and had three triangular, or lateen, **masts**.

Santa María de la Consolación

The *Santa María de la Consolación* was a huge ship known as a carrack. This was Ponce de León's flagship during his first voyage to Florida, which means that this was the boat that sailed with the Spanish flag at the front, or prow. The *Santa María de la Consolación* was built for carrying cargo and passengers. Merchants often used carracks for hauling large quantities of goods to and from trading ports. The *Santa María de la Consolación* could carry up to 38 people, while the *Santiago* could carry only about 20.

San Cristóbal

The *San Cristóbal* was the smallest of Ponce de León's ships. Known as a bergantina, this boat was sometimes powered by oars rather than by sails. It carried only about 15 people, but its size made it good for sailing close to shore and up rivers to explore.

(background) This illustration from 1502 shows the variety of different sizes and shapes of caravels.

Life at Sea

Terrible food, boredom, and serious illnesses were all difficulties at sea. To maintain order and make voyages run as smoothly as possible, sailors had very specific duties to follow.

Positions Onboard

The captain held the most important position aboard the ship. Ponce de León was captain on both voyages to Florida. He decided what responsibilities to assign the crew. All members of the crew answered to him, and anyone who disobeyed the captain's orders was punished. Punishments included **flogging**, being assigned a lower rank, or even death.

Surgeons and Medicine

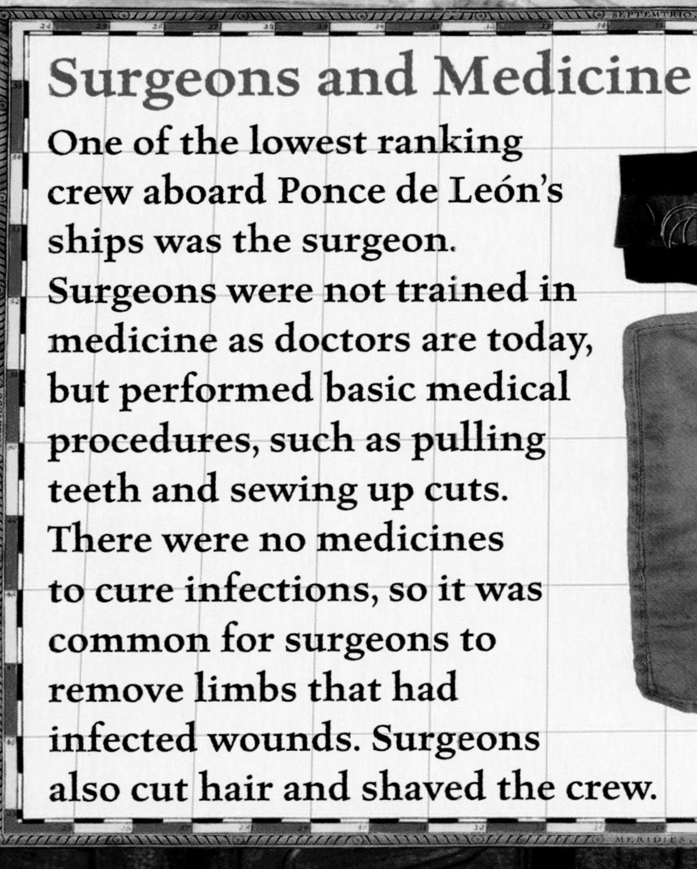

One of the lowest ranking crew aboard Ponce de León's ships was the surgeon. Surgeons were not trained in medicine as doctors are today, but performed basic medical procedures, such as pulling teeth and sewing up cuts. There were no medicines to cure infections, so it was common for surgeons to remove limbs that had infected wounds. Surgeons also cut hair and shaved the crew.

(background) The crew fought against rough seas and storms, such as hurricanes, often risking shipwreck and death. The seafaring diet did not include fresh fruits and vegetables, so many sailors developed scurvy, a disease that caused their gums to turn black and their teeth to fall out. Fleas living on rats aboard the ships carried more serious diseases.

Sweet Cassava Bread

Ponce de León grew cassava on his Puerto Rico plantation. Cassava was an ideal food for long voyages because it did not spoil in the moist sea air as many foods did. Ask an adult to help you make cassava bread.

Ingredients:

2 cups (500 mL) finely grated cassava
1 tsp (5 mL) salt
1/2 cup (125 mL) shredded coconut
1/2 cup (125 mL) brown sugar

Instructions:

1. Mix the cassava and salt. Place in a paper towel and squeeze out all of the liquid.
2. Spread half of the cassava in a frying pan.
3. Cover with coconut and brown sugar.
4. Spread the rest of the cassava on top and pat down.
5. Bake at 350°F (175°C) for about 20 minutes, or until the bread is lightly browned.
6. Wait until the bread has cooled before eating.

- Logbooks -
Pilots kept logs that described the areas they traveled to, weather conditions, and types of wildlife. They also recorded information on water color and temperature, and whether or not currents helped or hindered the ship.

- Compass -
The compass helped sailors to determine direction.

The Taino

The Taino Indians lived on several islands in the West Indies, including Hispaniola and Puerto Rico. Historians believe that the Taino welcomed the Spaniards when they first arrived. The Taino helped guide the Spanish ships safely to shore and traded their gold jewelry for the glass beads and bells that the Spanish offered them.

Taino Homes

Some historians believe there were as many as one million Taino living on Hispaniola before the Spanish arrived. Up to 600,000 Taino lived on the islands of Puerto Rico and Jamaica.

Clothing

Taino men wore loincloths made of cotton. Women wore short skirts also made of cotton. The Taino pierced their ears and noses and decorated their piercings with feathers and beads. They also wore belts and necklaces that were decorated with beads, feathers, gold, and shells. Village chiefs wore headdresses made of feathers and gold. Ponce de León and his men thought there was gold to be found on Puerto Rico when they saw that the Taino decorated themselves with gold ornaments.

Everyday Life

The Taino were farmers. They grew cassava and sweet potato, or batata, on mounds of earth called *conuco*. Crops grown on the *conuco* were easier to weed and harvest than crops grown on flat ground. The mounds also improved drainage, as rainwater ran down the mounds and prevented flooding. The Spaniards were quick to adopt this style of farming on their own settlements. Some other important food crops were squash, beans, peppers, peanuts, and maize, or corn. The Taino caught and ate fish in nets woven from palm tree leaves. They also killed and ate manatees, large sea animals, as well as iguanas, or lizards, that they hunted from the trees.

(background) A modern-day reconstruction of a Taino village. The Taino lived in houses built from wooden posts. Thatch made from grass and mud was used to make roofing. The homes were either round or rectangular and shad dirt floors. The Taino lived in villages of 20 to 50 houses each.

Calusa Encounters

Not all historians agree on where Ponce de León landed in Florida. Florida was inhabited by many different groups of American Indians, each with their own territory. Some think that the Calusa Indians attacked Ponce de León and his crew.

The Shell Indians

The Calusa Indians lived in the southwestern region of the Florida peninsula. They hunted and fished for food along the coasts. The Calusa are sometimes called the Shell Indians, because they made weapons, tools, jewelry, and sometimes even houses from conch shells and the shells of **crustaceans** that they ate. The Spaniards described the Calusa as being fierce and war-like, but many historians believe that the Calusa were protecting their territory by attacking the Spanish and preventing them from coming ashore.

(below) There are no historical drawings of the Calusa Indians. Other Florida Indians, such as the Timucua from northeast Florida, grilled and ate alligator, snakes, and fish.

(above) Florida Indians crafted large canoes up to 15 feet (five meters) long. The canoes were made from hollowed-out cypress or pine trees and used for traveling on the ocean. It is believed that the Calusa traveled as far as Cuba by canoe to trade.

Everyday Life

The Calusa built their homes on stilts so they would be safe from rising tides and flooding from the sea. Their homes did not have walls, and they made roofs by weaving together palm fronds, or leaves. The Calusa made spears from shell and fish bone to hunt eels, turtles, and deer. Women and children caught shellfish such as crabs, lobsters, and clams. Deerskin was used to make clothing. Women also wore dresses that were made from woven palm fronds and moss. Shells and small pieces of gold were used to decorate the belts they wore.

(right) The Calusa made tools, weapons, and jewelry from conch shells. Conch shells are the abandoned homes of sea animals called mollusks.

Contact

On Ponce de León's way back from his first trip to Florida, a skirmish occurred between the Spanish crew and the Calusa Indians. A fleet of 80 canoes carrying Calusa warriors rowed out to sea and attacked the Spanish ships. The Calusa's bows and arrows were no match for the Spanish harquebuses, and the Calusa eventually retreated.

After the Expeditions

After Ponce de León's voyages, Spanish settlers continued to come to the New World, some of them landing in Puerto Rico to continue to colonize the island. The city of Ponce, Puerto Rico, was founded in 1670, and was named after the first governor of the island.

(background) After Ponce de León was hit by a Calusa's poisoned arrow, he was taken to the nearest Spanish settlement at present-day Havana on the island of Cuba. His wound became infected, and the Spanish did not have medicines to treat it. Ponce de León died within weeks. He was 47 years old.

Taino Enslavement

Spanish colonists in Puerto Rico and on other Caribbean islands, forced the Taino to work in Spanish fields and to pan for gold. In return, the Taino were promised protection from the Carib Indians who lived on nearby islands. Many Taino starved because they were so busy working in Spanish fields that they did not have the time to tend their own crops. The Spaniards also tried to convert the Taino Indians to Christianity and force them to give up their traditional beliefs. Most Taino were unhappy under Spanish rule, and some rebelled. The Taino fought using clubs, spears, and bows and arrows. With these weapons, the Taino fought against the Spanish and were eventually overcome.

Fatal Diseases

Diseases introduced by the Spanish, such as measles, influenza, and smallpox, also killed many Taino Indians. The Taino had not been exposed to these diseases before, so they had no **immunity** against them, or the medicines to treat them. These illnesses were highly **contagious**, so they passed quickly from village to village. Entire villages were wiped out by diseases.

The Calusa's End

The Calusa suffered a similar fate as the Taino, except they were able to defend themselves against the Europeans for a little while longer. Aside from European diseases, many Calusa died at the hands of enemy tribes of present-day Georgia and South Carolina. These neighboring peoples raided Calusa territory in brutal attacks that left many dead.

Parceling out land

During colonization, conquistadors in Puerto Rico and Hispaniola established a system of landholding called the *encomienda* system. An *encomienda* was land granted to the explorer who discovered it that included at least one Indian village. Groups of 30 to 80 Indians were also granted to be used as slaves on the land. Conquistadors were rewarded an *encomienda* for duties that they performed for the Spanish king, such as putting down a rebellion. Ponce de León was rewarded an *encomienda* in Hispaniola for his leadership in a war against rebelling Taino at Higüey, Hispaniola, in 1511.

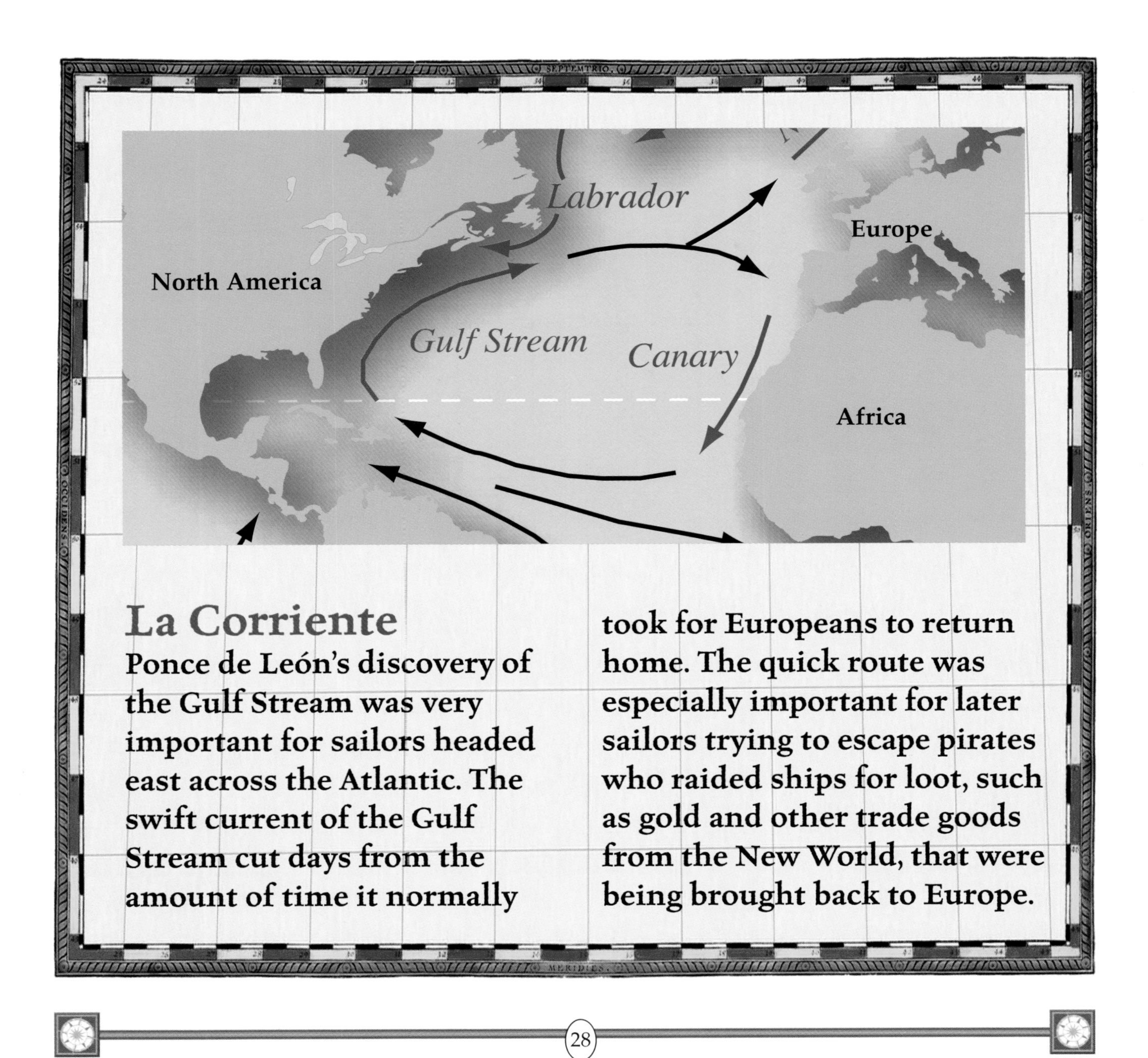

La Corriente

Ponce de León's discovery of the Gulf Stream was very important for sailors headed east across the Atlantic. The swift current of the Gulf Stream cut days from the amount of time it normally took for Europeans to return home. The quick route was especially important for later sailors trying to escape pirates who raided ships for loot, such as gold and other trade goods from the New World, that were being brought back to Europe.

(background) Ponce de León was not successful in establishing a Spanish colony at La Florida. Many of the colonists who accompanied him on the second expedition were killed in the Calusa attack. The survivors of the attack abandoned the dream of building a colony in Florida and joined another conquistador, Hernando Cortés, in Mexico. A Spanish colony was not established in Florida for another 38 years.

Ponce de León's Legacy

Ponce de León was a loyal Spanish soldier and stern military commander who was well rewarded in the New World. He founded a successful settlement in Puerto Rico, and is credited as the Spanish discoverer of Florida.

Puerto Rico Today

The Taino Indians eventually disappeared from the Caribbean Islands, but their culture still remains. Several towns in Puerto Rico have kept their original Taino names, including Coamo and Mayagüez. Hammocks and barbecues were Taino inventions that are today used all over the world. Today, Spanish is Puerto Rico's official language and Roman Catholicism, the religion brought by the Spanish, is the main religion.

(left) A sign for a tourist attraction in Florida today. Florida also has a strong Spanish heritage, in part because of Ponce de León's voyages there.

Was Ponce the First to Explore Florida?

Some historians believe that there were voyages to Florida before Ponce de León officially discovered it. Expeditions during the 1500s had to be approved by the Spanish king beforehand so that explorers could earn funding. Still, unofficial voyages were common, in which explorers searched for land to be sure that it existed before approaching the king with the request to seek new territory. By doing this, explorers rarely disappointed their kings by returning empty-handed.

Probanzas and the Spanish Conquest

The role of the conquistadors in the Spanish conquest of the New World is debated by historians today. The main sources of information about the conquest are first-hand reports written by the conquistadors and their men, which were sent back to the Spanish king. These reports, called probanzas, were written to prove to the king that the conqueror deserved rewards, such as titles and pensions, for their work. Some historians today question the facts presented by the conquistadors in these reports, and the role that individuals played in the conquest. The information on events and people in this book are based on the probanzas and some historians' interpretations of these reports.

Artwork

There were no cameras or video recording equipment during the Spanish conquest. The artwork in this book was created later by artists who were not present at the events. For this reason, the events may not have happened exactly as they appear in this book, but in styles that were popular during an artist's lifetime.

(right) A statue of Ponce de León, Puerto Rico's first governor, stands in Old San Juan, Puerto Rico.

Glossary

cargo The supplies of a ship

Christian A follower of the teachings of Jesus Christ

coat-of-arms A symbol that identified an important person or family in the Middle Ages, the period in European history from about 500 A.D. to 1500

colonize To take over a land that is not one's own and rule over its resources and people

contagious Able to spread easily and quickly

convert To change one's religion, faith, or beliefs

crustacean A water animal that has no backbone and is covered in a hard shell

fertile Able to produce abundant crops or vegetation

flogging A beating, usually with a whip or strap

governor An official who oversees a territory

Gulf Stream A warm ocean current that flows through the Atlantic Ocean

immunity The body's natural ability to fight off sickness

inheritance Money, property, or titles received after a person's death

Islam A religion in which followers believe in one god, *Allah*, and follow the teachings of the prophet Muhammad

knight A soldier from the Middle Ages who fought on horseback

masts Vertical poles that support sails on a ship

navigate To direct the course, or direction, of a ship

New World The name given to North, Central, and South America by Europeans after they discovered that these lands existed

ocean current A large body of warm or cold water that moves around the oceans in a continuous path

peninsula A piece of land that juts out into a body of water

pilot The person who steers a ship

plantation A large farm that usually grows only one type of crop and employs a large number of workers

rebellion An uprising against a ruler

recruit To get a person to join in

staple A main part

Index